SINGLE IS NOT A CURSE

Tony A. Gaskins, Jr.

Library of Congress Cataloging-in-Publication Data

Tony A. Gaskins Jr.,
Single Is Not A Curse
Edited by: Jenna Cabbell
Published by: Soul Writers, LLC: PO Box 291835 Tampa, FL 33687

Library of Congress Control Number:

ISBN:9780615916644

10 9 8 7 6 5 4 3 2 1

Printed in the United States of America

Note: This book is intended only as an informative guide for those wishing to know about love. Readers are advised to consult a professional relationship coach or counselor before making any changes in their love life. The reader assumes all responsibility for the consequences of any actions taken based on the information presented in this book. The information in this book is based on the author's research and experience. Every attempt has been made to ensure that the information is accurate; however, the author cannot accept liability for any errors that may exist. The facts and theories on love and relationships are subject to interpretation, and the conclusions and recommendations presented here may not agree with other interpretations.

Contents

✦ Introduction ✦

AS A MARRIED relationship coach, I often find myself coaching singles on how to find and maintain a marriage. I have discovered that the majority of singles do not desire to be single, and many actually despise single life. Some, however, have reached a place of acceptance for singlehood and have learned to embrace everything that comes along with it.

As a married man, I learned in marriage what I wish I had learned while single. Marriage taught me how to appreciate single life and see it as a training ground. I received the wrong training during my single years, and paid the price after wedlock; those overdue lessons nearly ruined my marriage.

I was sitting up late one evening having a discussion with my wife about how there are so many single and unhappy people out in the world. We are both frequently bombarded with questions from singles. That conversation sparked the fire for me to pen this book. I'm writing this book for all singles and those who are preparing to end toxic relationships to be single again. I want to help you see the beauty and benefits of single life and utilize it to the fullest. I also want to prepare you for lasting love.

Single life is the training ground; it is imperative that you are training the right way. It would be impossible for me to cover every aspect of single life in extensive detail, but I will provide you with solid fundamentals in hopes that this can help you not only find peace while single, but also attract real love if that is what you truly desire. If you have flipped through any of my previous books, then you know that I don't pull punches. So take a deep breath, get a pen and pad, and let's go to work! Remember, I'm not a Journalism major; I'm a servant. My writing style is not by the book, but I write from my heart. Understand that!

Why Are You Single?

I KNOW A LOT of singles who despise being asked, "Why are you single?" Well, it's a necessary question. You will do yourself a huge favor by asking it. If you are single for reasons beyond your control or your knowledge and are 100% fine with your status, then great. If you are not happy being single, then you need to find out what actions you can take to attract the love of your life.

It is critical that you do not lie to yourself. We sometimes tell ourselves that we do not want something because we cannot attain it at the moment. That is a huge mistake, but it's practically human nature. To soothe our emotional wounds, we try to convince ourselves that we do not want love and that love isn't for everybody. That mindset is dangerous. It's dangerous because you actually begin to believe that lie. Unfortunately, in this case, you will attract into your life what you believe. If you believe that love is not for you, then your face and demeanor will express that without you even realizing it.

Just be honest about the question and if there is something in your power that you can change, change it. If there is nothing in your power that you can change, it's a sign that it is simply not your time and your focus should be on other aspects of your life. You just have to figure out your answer and then take action.

I work with clients who seem well-rounded and perfectly ready for love but still cannot seem to attract it. Even though there may be no obvious flaws, they still fail to find lifelong mates. They believe there is very little they can change about themselves; when people feel this way, it is vital for them to fulfill other areas in life. To be prepared to embark on a loving relationship with another person, it is essential to answer one's true calling. Many times people will ignore their personal callings; yet prematurely answer the call to love. As a result, they never get to fulfill their own purpose because it was derailed. Many people want love so desperately that they attract it before attracting their dreams, and sometimes having both fails to work out as smoothly as they had hoped.

It is almost impossible for a person to have absolutely nothing to work on while in waiting. None of us are perfect, so there is always something that can be done physically, mentally and/or emotionally. The key is to recognize that and then take action. I have noticed our world growing more and more superficial than ever before. Everything is based on looks, tastes, style, sexual attraction and material possessions. With social media buzzing like crazy and a plethora of fake "reality" TV shows airing each day, our world has become highly sexually charged. I have tried many times to match couples that are seemingly perfect, both spiritually and emotionally – but then one of them does not like something physical about the other person. In my experience as a relationship coach, I have come to find that many people want others who simply do not want them back. What's worse is that these people are clueless to the fact that the affection is not mutual, so they expend more and more effort trying to attract a certain "type" and it never comes to fruition.

Women tend to be picky about the types of men they will date, and men are even pickier. If I survey a wise woman, I find that she will eventually take a chance on a guy she would not normally date. I can have that same type of talk with a man, and he will not budge on what he likes. The sad part is that what he likes, might not like him back. That is typically the case, and it goes both ways.

My grandmother had a saying: "Like who likes you, not who you like." Now that cannot be taken literally in every sense, but in its purest form it means that you should appreciate someone who appreciates you. Ordinarily a person wants someone who is a "trophy" piece; there is a failure to realize that the "trophy" sees the other person as just a "shelf" and not as another trophy. Why do we operate this way?

A doctor could probably provide a clinical explanation, but I'll give you a practical explanation from my findings as a relationship coach. Oftentimes, an individual wants someone who will grant them approval. We typically want mates who are out of our league. We desire those who we adore, admire and idolize because if they reciprocate those feelings, then we will feel validated in life. We seek approval of others, and someone who is gorgeous or has higher status can grant that approval if they like us the way we like them. That is where the problem lies.

There is someone who looks up to you, but you are probably looking down on him or her. There is someone who you look up to and that same person is probably looking down on you. Do you remember seeing in movies how the genius, quiet guy with the big glasses always coveted the beautiful cheerleader who initially didn't even know he existed? That is art imitating life. That is the premise for so many movies because the same scenario occurs in our everyday lives. On the other hand, there is the quiet, plain-Jane female who adores the muscular jock. Why is that?

Usually, a person does not want to be with an individual who is a reflection of self because it's a harsh realization of how unhappy one is with life. Therefore, many people desire counterparts whom they see as upgrades in order to make themselves feel better. Take some time and sit with that thought for a moment. If it is true, I know the reality of it stings. If it is not true for you, then I'm sure you have seen it in someone else.

To paint a more vivid picture, I will give you a real-life example. Imagine that I am coaching a guy who stands 6' tall and weighs roughly 350 pounds. Let's say he is a great guy and is looking for love. Now imagine that when I ask him what type of woman he wants, he describes an exotic beauty. He claims that he wants a woman who stands under 6' tall and weighs less than 175 pounds. Trust me, it happens every day.

So, I go out and find a woman who looks like what he desires. Then I connect the two of them. He falls in love with her looks right away, and even her personality flaws seem beautiful because he is enamored with her looks. On the other hand, she loves his personality but she is not as equally fond of his looks and size because she sees him as disproportionate in height and weight. When I ask her to describe her own "type," she describes him as taller than her, even when she wears her heels, with an athletically built body. Her description sounds like that of a professional athlete or of a guy who played collegiate sports.

So this 6' tall, 350-pound man wants her, but she has her eyes set on a guy who is 6'4" and weighs approximately 185-210 pounds, ripped in muscle. The one thing that she is usually willing to accept in place of physical attraction is if he makes over $300,000 a year, which is the typical pro-athlete salary. Now, if I have a talk with her and give her real facts, she may feel guilty for being superficial and may be willing to give the shorter, heavier guy a chance. Conversely, the guy does not really want to hear any explanations as to why he cannot have his dream girl. So now we have a woman who feels like she's settling and a man who won't be satisfied – because if he does get this beautiful woman whom he's not accustomed to having, he will most likely grow complacent and take her for granted instead of appreciating her (unless he's matured already).

This scenario continues. Imagine the woman gets tired of settling for the short guy, has decided that she wants the 6'4" guy, and I go find him. Then I introduce her to the 6'4" guy and she falls madly in love with him because he fits the image of her dream. To him, she may be just another woman because he's accustomed to women clamoring over his height and good looks. So now, she sees him as a "trophy" and he sees her as a "shelf." The only way he sees her as a "trophy" is if she is absolutely gorgeous to him. If he is mature enough, then he might appreciate her; but once again, only if she is absolutely gorgeous.

So I ask you: Is the short, heavy guy wrong for wanting a sexy, built, beautiful woman? Is the sexy, built woman wrong for not wanting the short, nice guy? Is the woman wrong for wanting a 6'4" guy who sees her as just another woman? Who's to blame? How can we fix this?

Those scenarios are why millions of people are single today. Many want partners who do not want them back. You have to ask yourself: Are you a part of the problem or the solution? Rarely do we want our equal; we always want someone seemingly of a higher caliber than us. There are a lot of women who make $60,000 or less annually but only want to date men with annual incomes of $100,000 or more. Is he wrong for not wanting her because she is not on his financial level? Is she wrong for wanting a man who makes more than she does? Can you blame him for wanting a woman with an annual income of $100,000 or more who matches his earnings, as long as he's man enough to handle it?

This is what I find every day and this is what needs to be understood. Who are you looking down on and why? Someone likes you and wants to be with you, but why don't you want to reciprocate? There are a million reasons, I know. But you know the difference between a good reason and a bad reason. If it's a good reason then you do not have to confront this, but if it is a bad reason, then you really need to evaluate it. A bad reason is because the person is too short, too heavy, does not have the exact features of your dreams, or lacks the annual income you desire. Those are all bad reasons. A good reason is because this person is controlling, irresponsible, abusive, unfaithful, untrustworthy, etc. Identify your reasons for not wanting the person who wants you and make sure they are good reasons.

If each person does this and you share this book with as many people as you know, then we start to make a change in our world. Share it with the person whom you may want, but for some reason does not act like the feeling is mutual. Share it with that friend who always desires someone unrealistic or out of reach, like the single woman in the small town who is waiting on a Prince Charming from a big city to come sweep her off her feet because she thinks that is what God promised her in a dream. You have to be real with yourself first.

If you are single for a good reason, then embrace this singlehood. It is a blessing, not a curse! If you are single because you left a toxic relationship, then great! If you are single because you are working on yourself to get to where you need to be, then great! If you are single because of school, work, or your children are the main areas of your focus right now, then great! If you are single just because you have not met the one who is for you and you are being completely honest with yourself about what you want in a partner, then great! Be single for a good reason! Be single for a real reason!

Don't be single just because you are too picky. Don't let it be because you are turning down everyone who wants you due to a physical attribute or superficial characteristic. More men are guilty of that than women, I must admit. If you know you are superficial and you're coming to terms with it, right now I want you to know that numbers cannot measure love. Attributes like height, weight and salary cannot measure or predict love. Anyone can lose weight, anyone can learn how to earn more money, and regardless of a person's looks or height, they can love you like you deserve to be loved! See the bigger picture and make sure you are not single for the wrong reasons!

Recall the last person you dated or the last person who showed genuine interest in you. Use the space below to list why it did not work out.

Now read back through your explanation and ask yourself if your singlehood is due to good reasons or bad reasons. Be honest with yourself and in your answer. Change your answer if you feel like you were not totally honest. If your answer was because there was no chemistry or physical attraction, then I really want you to think about that and ask yourself just how deeply important that is to you. How long are you willing to wait to meet that person with whom you share deep physical attraction? Also consider the fact that the person you are physically attracted to may not feel the same way about you.

Please understand that I am not asking you to settle. I am asking you not to confuse standards with preferences. What you want and what you need may be two different things, but what you want and what you need should be the same things. Want what you need, not what you want.

If you read your reason as to why your last love connection did not work and you know it was for good reason, then smile and be happy about that. It's good that you did not settle for someone who is abusive, controlling, empty, vain, lazy, or anything else along those lines. It is not your job to raise or change anyone. It is the other person's job to read a book like this and implement some type of self-improvement.

Take the time to write down the characteristics you are looking for in a partner.

Now, look back at your list and see how many of those traits are statistics like height, weight, salary, etc. Hopefully, by this point, there aren't many. If there are, then really think about those stipulations and examine how long you have been waiting on them. Are these requisites absolutely necessary to have? If it is necessary to have everything on your list, ask yourself how long you are willing to wait for them. Please make sure you are waiting for the right reasons and that they are absolutely worth the wait. If you are waiting to meet someone who makes a certain amount of money or is a certain height, those are not good reasons to wait, in my opinion. Why? Because you can find someone with those things who still turns out to be a bad person, which will result in settling or waiting even more years to meet another person with those superficial specifications.

Let's re-examine your entire list of requirement for a partner. Including everything you can think of, now make a list of the top things that you feel you are willing to compromise.

Make sure that nothing listed is related to character, dignity, integrity or faith. You should never compromise foundational necessities. It is okay to compromise tangible attributes, but do not compromise the intangibles.

The goal of those exercises is to get you thinking about what really matters regarding your choice of a partner and to eliminate the traits that do not really matter. No one should be single for the wrong reasons while longing for a love that really is not based on true love.

Single Life Is Not A Curse

MANY WILL NOT truthfully admit that they feel single life is a curse. There are times that you may feel like God or society has forgotten you and that you might die lonely. Sometimes you feel that if it has not happened in all of these years, then what is going to be different about the next 10 or 20 years? You say to yourself, *I've done all that I know how to do and still nothing has happened for me in the love department.* You have hopes and dreams that you would like to fulfill, but many days, you feel that you would rather achieve them with your partner than by yourself.

There are some nights that you either laid in bed and stared at the ceiling or cried on your pillow, wondering when love would come. You have prayed about it, meditated about it, read all types of books about it, changed the TV shows you watch, changed the music you play and still struggle with finding peace in your singlehood. It hurts, I know. The pain of singleness caused me to enter many toxic relationships that caused a lot of pain. It is human nature to fight the feeling or to run from it. Running from it means that you are running into any relationship just to prevent feeling lonely. Fighting it means that you make the best of it no matter what stress may come your way.

Single life is a gift! There is good in single life. First, try to list at least 5 things that you enjoy about single life!

Now really ponder on those things and embrace them. If your list is empty, we have some problems. I know many singles say they appreciate not having to answer to anyone and being able to hang with their friends whenever they want. Those things do change when in a relationship, so it's good to embrace that freedom while you are still single.

To be realistic, I know there are some things you dislike about single life and I want you to list those things below.

My hope is that you have a longer list of things you like about single life than the list of your dislikes about single life. If not, then we will keep working!

Understand that if you are taking care of yourself, then you should have a long life ahead of you. As you may already know, it is challenging to live with someone else. There are a lot of compromises that need to be made and a lot of personal changes must be made as well. The beauty of single life is that you only have to please yourself. While you are single, you get to do what you want to do. You have the liberty to focus on whatever you choose. There are gifts! I want to share those gifts with you, and I want you to grasp these gifts and appreciate them while you can. If you desire love, I urge you to put what you learn in this book into action, and I don't think you will be single much longer.

The Five F's:

1.) Freedom

When you are single, you get to experience true freedom. If you do not have children, then you really have the luxury of freedom. But even if you do have children, there is still a level of independence that does not exist in a relationship. When you are single, you can spontaneously get up and go whenever you want to, you can eat what you want, you can spend what you want, and you can leave your home as messy or as neat as you want. You call all the shots.

We always think that the grass is greener on the other side, but it has been taught that the grass is greener where you water it. It is imperative that you embrace that concept. It is important for you to realize that this freedom will not last always, and as soon as tomorrow approaches, your freedom could start to change. Instead of desiring what you do not have, you must appreciate what you *do* have. You have to utilize your freedom of choice as if you will lose it tomorrow. You must be present, live in the moment and enjoy what you have. Do something today just because you can!

Drink the last bit of milk, eat the last snack, go on a joy ride, plan a vacation, write and execute a bucket list and splurge on something you really want, not because you need it, but because you simply want it. Utilize your freedom because you will not have this type of freedom forever. Trust me, your freedom will change!

Right now, you are probably saying that you do all those things already and you're tired of it and would rather do them with someone you love. Yes, you may have already been doing them, but not with a smile on your face while being present. You may have been doing them but – instead of being present – your mind is in the future while you are doing those things, and that anticipation is stealing the joy from the moment. Stop fantasizing about what you do not have and appreciate what you *do* have.

2.) Focus

The focus that you can have in single life is unparalleled by any other type of focus. You can focus on whatever you want to and no one can stop you. Focus on your faith and build it! If you want to write a book, start a foundation, travel around the world, start a business, or grow spiritually, you can do it now! When you are engrossed in a relationship, your focus is split; that is very frustrating at times because someone else needs you when you need yourself.

Choose something to focus on and – whatever it is – make sure that you are so focused that you can become the best at it. While you are working on it, refrain from wishing that you had someone with whom to share it. Focus on it with the intent to be the best who has ever done it, and build it knowing that whomever you end up with will respect, admire and appreciate you for that focus. This is very important: having focus can actually attract your partner. You are always sexier to the person whom you're trying to attract when you are focused. It is human nature to be attracted to ambition. Well, ambition requires focus! You cannot be ambitious if you lack focus. Instead of drooling over a partner, smile over your work! When your potential life-partner is watching you from a distance, you will look much better if you're smiling over your work instead of drooling over them.

Think about it. It has always been said that love comes when you least expect it. You will "least expect it" when you are fully focused on something else. If someone wants you and is worth your time, then this individual will distract you from that focus at the right time. On the other side, you will not even notice the existence of someone who is not worth it.

This is why you see so many people end up with counterparts who are not even worth their time. The problem is they were not focused on anything that contributed to their personal growth, and as a result they just accepted whatever or whomever they could get. When you have that laser-beam focus, it is much easier to tell if someone is serious about you or not! Your vision becomes so keen that you can see right through someone who is full of it! Find something positive to channel your focus, and let it guide you. This is how you will attract your love.

There are many people who were possibly overlooked because of physical reasons or financial reasons or whatever reasons, but as soon as they became focused on one thing and began to build it and perfect it, they attracted real love. Focus is sexy!!

3.) Family

In your single life, your family is a gift. You should perfect your relationship with your family. Whoever they are, be sure to draw closer to them and nurture those relationships. It could be your mother, father, sibling, best friend, or anyone you consider family. Make sure that your bond is strengthened and that real love is formed within your circle of trusted loved ones. Also, make them aware and prepare them for the day when things will change when you attract your true love. Your bond with them will not alter, but help them to understand that how you spend your time will need to adjust.

A lot of people never really build those family bonds because they are always looking for love. They wait until they attract toxic love to start trying to build with family for the purpose of refuge and attention. That is backwards. Instead, use single life as a gift; use that time to build a bond so strong with your family so that when you attract real love, they understand how you must split your time. They will also know that if you ever want to talk or need them in a serious way, you will call them. You also know that they will be there for you no matter what because you have built such a strong bond.

Women love talking to their mothers or their girlfriends every day. Well, it's important that you do that now while you are single so that when you attract love, you don't have to do it as much and take away important time from your lover. This has damaged many relationships because one partner did not know how to be in a relationship with a lover, and instead was involved in a "love triangle" with family and the significant other. That cannot happen and it will not work. So embrace the single life now and take advantage of the fact that you can call your mom or friend anytime you want, that you are free from worrying about splitting your time, and that the people around you will not feel any less loved.

4.) Finances

In this single season, you can focus on your finances. What I mean is that you should try to make as much money as you can and build your credit to absolute perfection. It will be challenging but fun at the same time. Many people miss out on opportunities because they are so preoccupied with looking for love that they miss the money they could be earning. Make money now so that when you meet your love, you have the means to make real-life decisions like traveling the world or starting a family. Make money now so that you can bring something to the table. Make money now so that even if your next relationship fails, you have the means to break free and fall back on a savings. Make money that will be yours and only yours. Don't make money to give it away to a boyfriend who doesn't even really love you. Make money for you, and keep that money until you know you have absolutely found the love of your life, you have a ring and a commitment, and he has put in enough time that you can trust he will not turn into a monster.

Work on your credit so that you have a good name. Many people make the mistake of going into debt and ruining their credit while single because they are trying to buy happiness during singleness. Instead of being able to buy happiness, they actually purchase misery. This can actually deter love because for some people, poor credit is a deal breaker. You cannot blame someone for not wanting to be with you if your credit is horrible due to simple greed or irresponsibility. People have the right to protect their personal assets, future and names. So use this time now to prepare for your love by making sure your name is in good enough standing to join with a potential partner.

5.) Friends

In your single life, you must embrace your friends! This is the time to embrace your old friends and make new friends. You need people who will be genuinely happy for you when you attract real love. You also need a circle of loved ones to help you get through the rough times when you're down about single life. You need a support network that is not going to keep you down but aims to help you get up. You need friends. In a relationship, you may not be able to maintain that level of closeness to your friends because your partner will become your best friend. So appreciate the friendships while you can!!

Don't sit with your friends and sulk over not having anyone to love. Instead, enjoy the guys' or girls' nights out, laugh, talk, smile, and have fun because at some point, all of this will have to shift to accommodate your future relationship. The conversations, the locations, and the frequency will all change when you attract love! In this time, it is crucial for you to find a way to love your friends and love your current position. Instead of picturing your partner while you are with your friends, picture the fact that one day, you may have to sacrifice some of the time spent with them, and then begin to embrace the moment. As stated earlier, be present!

Those are the 5 F's of single life! Remember those gifts and embrace them. Stop wishing you had something that you don't and start appreciating what you *do* have. That will make a huge difference in your life. Single life is not a curse; it is a gift.

How To Love Yourself

The Three B's

LOVING YOURSELF DOES not equate to being complacent. Loving you means working on yourself. I call it the Three B's:

BRAIN:

In this space of singleness, you need to feed your mind. Refrain from consuming so many junk reality TV shows. Discipline yourself. Feed your mind with things that will actually help you! Use this space to learn everything there is to learn about you, about love, and about relationships.

Let's start with you. You need to learn what you do wrong in relationships. Learn what buttons you push and which mistakes you make. We all need work. No human is perfect. There are many times a woman hires me for life coaching and complains to me about all the things her ex did wrong. However, in that process I also hear a lot of things she did wrong that she has never considered. Therefore, since she came to me for help, it is not my place to harp on all the things her ex did wrong or I would be saying the same things her family and friends have been telling her. I point out the things she could have done differently to generate a better outcome. I show her the mirror and ask her to confront herself first.

The beauty about confronting yourself is that when you change, the types of men you attract will change. When you learn what behaviors to reinforce and what behaviors to stop, then you change the dynamics of a relationship and you begin to get different results from your man. Sometimes you create the monster you are dealing with by what you allow, what you stop and what you reinforce. One of my quotes is floating all over the internet, and it says:

> *You teach people how to treat you by what you allow, what you stop, and what you reinforce.*
> *~Tony A Gaskins Jr*

If you have seen that and did not know it was mine, now you do. I wrote that because I noticed so many women who were in bad relationships because they reinforced "grown-boy" behaviors from the start; as a result, the behaviors only got worse. On top of that, many women have "grown-girl" behaviors that further create monsters.

There are many women who love to play detective in their relationships. This is one of the biggest mistakes a woman can make for many reasons. One reason is because if you seek, you shall find. If you go digging for dirt, then everyone will always be dirty. Another reason is because you then put your man into game or competition mode, which causes him to step up his cheating ways instead of letting them go. He steps up because now it seems as if you are challenging him. If there is any "grown-boy" in him, you have opened the door for him to release those negative behaviors. Now he *wants* to cheat to spite you for invading his privacy. In addition, he is now curious to see if he is good enough to beat the "law." You are his detective Columbo, and now his goal is to outsmart you.

Whereas on the other hand, if you just trust that any wrongdoings in the dark will come to the light, you can live in peace instead of being on edge every day thinking every other woman wants your man. Please do not interpret my message as a suggestion for you to play the fool. What I'm saying is don't *be* a fool and create problems that may not even exist.

When you are a confident and strong woman, that confidence and strength is so sexy to a man that it makes him fall in love. The reason is because these attributes make you different from other women. You are the woman who does not feel the need to check phones, receipts, Facebook, Twitter and Instagram. You are a woman who knows who you are and what you stand for and you have enough confidence to know what you bring to the table. You also know that if he is foolish enough to cheat on you, then he deserves to lose you. You are sure that just like you got him, you can certainly replace him.

While you are walking in this confidence, it confuses the man because he is accustomed to needy and insecure women. Now he is infatuated with your strength and perplexed by it. So instead of cheating, he wants to be close to you at all times. He clearly sees your worth and knows that if he will not be there for you, another man will. That is precisely how I am committed to my wife, because that is how she carries herself. I do not have time to cheat nor do I think of trying to cheat. I know what I have at home and that if I betrayed her trust, she would be gone in an instant and would not look back. She has let me know that over the years with her strength and poise. It is so intriguing to me that I would rather study her than study anyone else. So I can speak to this from a male's perspective; I live it every day.

After you have worked on yourself, it is time to acquire knowledge about love and relationships. The next "B" is the Brand.

BRAND:

Every woman needs a brand. What that means is that every woman needs a website. You should have a blog, a company, a mission, or something. If you don't have a .com, then you're not ready yet. It may sound simple or trivial, but it's actually very profound.

You see, your brand represents stability and independence. A man is looking for a woman who knows who she is, what she stands for, what she wants, and where she's going. The "grown-boys" are the ones who want you to be fully dependent on them. A real man wants you to have your own mission but still know when to support him on his. A real man does not want to rescue you; he wants to join you.

Your brand will represent independence, ambition, clarity, confidence, and courage. However, there is a fine line. The brand must be what you do, not who you are. That company and website that you build should not be your everything. It should be a part of you, but not you entirely. You should work your butt off for it, but you should not let the sweat show. It should not be the only area of your conversation and focus. A man wants a woman who is independent but ready to become interdependent. That means that you have built your brand to a point that it has legs and it can run itself or be easily managed. After a certain amount of building your brand, you should not have to work on it 16 hours a day. If that is still the case, then you are not relationship-ready. You still need to focus on you and build your brand.

You may have a great corporate job and be extremely happy with it. That's cool, too. Your job may work you to the bone, but that may be a problem for a man. He wants you to have a job, but he doesn't want the job to have you. It is natural for a man to be consumed with work and to work himself to the bone; that is not natural for a woman. A woman knows how to kick back, have a good time and how to separate work from home. Unfortunately, some women become naturals at working themselves to the bone while trying not to think about being single. Let's be honest. I coach women every day, so you do not have to fool yourself for me.

A man wants to know that you can also manage a home because your natural strengths allow you do that, whereas managing a home could drive him insane. He needs to know that you will not neglect the kids and the grease cooking on the stove so that you can kiss your boss's butt on the Blackberry all evening. Please don't confuse me here; I am not suggesting that you transform into a 1950s woman without any ambition, goals or career. I know that critics would love to debate this with the Women's Liberation movement. What I am suggesting is that you graduate to a point to where you can separate work from home.

Your aim should be for your boss to clearly understand the parameters of your hours; if you get paid for 8-10 hours a day, you should not have to put aside your duties at home to work beyond that. If it can't be done while at work, then it can't be done; if that is not good enough, you can either demand compensation for your overtime or simply let that company go, find another job or start your own company with your man supporting you.

So let's be clear: it is perfectly fine to work overtime, to work from home and to work all night if you are living in singlehood. If that's the space you are in and you are 100% happy and fulfilled in that space, then that is a sign that you probably should remain single, because you are married to the grind and there is no room for a man. But if that is what you are doing now because you do not have a man, then you need to know for sure you can adjust if your husband walks into your life. He will examine your life and if you are a slave to the job, then he won't stay. This is what is meant by "work your butt off, but don't show the sweat." To a man who is watching, you will look like a wife-in-waiting, not a slave to a job from which you will never break free. Build your career and build your brand, but do not let them consume you or control you. If you are controlled by your career, that is not happiness; that is expensive misery.

Even outside of your career or corporate job, you should have a brand. If your corporate job will not allow you to brand yourself, then at least create a blog. Empower yourself to have something that you own and can control. This should be something that shows you have interests and passions beyond work. A job can let you go, but a dream can't let you go because you hold it. Don't just have a job, have a dream.

Another aspect of the brand is how you dress and carry yourself. For most women, this is common sense and you do it the right way naturally. However, for others, it does not come as easily. It is important that you know not just the latest trends in fashion, but also what works for your body type. A man has no clue if you purchased your clothes from Neiman Marcus or The Goodwill. As long as you rock it well and wear it with confidence, then that is all that matters to him.

A lot of men pay attention to hair and nails as well. It's not about the style; it's about the presentation. Make sure that your hair and nails always look clean. That is a representation of how you take care of yourself. If you cannot afford the $60 every week or every two weeks for a manicure and pedicure, then get nail clippers, a fingernail file and nail polish from CVS and do your own nails. A man cannot tell the difference unless he is a man who gets his own nails done professionally. He just wants to see that your hands and feet are taken care of and that your hair is well-kept.

You are a woman, and you are the most resourceful being on the planet. Even if you cannot afford to dress in expensive, designer clothes and you cannot afford to visit the most upscale hair and nail salon in town, you are resourceful enough to make something out of nothing. You can do it; you just may not feel the desire to do it. But if you want to attract your husband, he will take notice of that.

Natural hair is currently a growing trend. That is perfectly fine; just wear your natural hair clean and well-kept. If you are wearing the 'fro, there is no need to have lint and debris in it. Also, I understand that returning to natural hair is a movement and that for many women; it serves the purpose of cleansing your mind, body and soul. Here is a tip for my natural women; go natural, but don't go bitter. I have met a lot of natural women who said some very mean and hurtful things to me about my ministry without ever really talking to me or hearing me out. You have to heal, you have to love, and you have to realize that no one is against you, trying to hurt you or forcing you to conform. You can be just as beautiful, and in many cases, even more beautiful than the women who use relaxers. You just have to exude confidence and radiance and not feel like everyone is staring at you and judging you. If you are going to be natural, then be happy and vibrantly natural, not bitter and confrontational.

BODY:

The body is very important because a man is a visual creature and your body will be among the first things he sees. Which body part do you think a man focuses on first? You've probably heard this before: one man may say he's a "leg man," while another is attracted to either a woman's breasts or behind (butt? Backside?). Still some men like long hair, a certain grade of hair, or a certain eye color. I'm not saying it's right for men to devote all of their attention to the physical, any more than it is right for you to do it. I'm just trying to arm you with the information. With that in mind, you may be surprised to find out the body part men focus on the most is a woman's stomach. Your stomach is what holds your food, and – unless you have a medical issue -- it is indicative of how much you eat. This is always a very sensitive issue for women because weight is a taboo topic. I cover this in my seminars, and I cringe before I do it. It hurts me to talk about weight as much as it hurts you to hear about weight.

Before anything else, your body is your brand. Your body tells a person how you take care of yourself. A man has a picture in his mind of what a healthy body looks like. That picture is unique to that man. What some men call a nice body, some women call "fat." I have seen this disparity firsthand.

I heard someone say once, "I have never eaten any-thing on accident." You have to ask yourself: Are you eating on accident and are you working out on purpose? Don't lose focus here. I am not setting a certain size or weight goal for you to reach. What I am asking you is if you are the CEO of your body. Are you managing your body the right way? Are you eating the right foods? Are you working out the right way? If a workout doesn't hurt and if you aren't seeing your body change, then you are doing the wrong workout.

Some people work out like they go to church; it's just a tradition.

You have to eat what you do not want to eat sometimes and work out when you do not want to work out in order to keep your body in shape. Don't kill yourself trying to get a man. Help yourself live by being healthy. That means by healthy eating and working out. Eat real meals, clean meals and do real workouts. The purpose is not to get your body to look like the next woman's body. The purpose is to get your body to the best shape possible for you. If that is 200 pounds, then that is okay. If that is 150 pounds, then be okay with that as well. Just know that you have taken care of your meal plan and workout plan to the best of your ability and that you are in absolutely the best place possible.

To be 100% honest, being out of shape is one of the top reasons that some women are unable to find men. It's also one of the top reasons many men aren't able to get the woman he wants.

Don't view this as a chore to be completed to cater to a man! Do this for yourself! Do this for your health and wellness as an individual. At the end of the day, what size you are is your choice, unless there is something medically wrong that will not allow you to lose weight or to be healthy. If you are heavier than most women, 100% healthy and you work out hard 3-6 times a week, then you are doing what you have to do!

The key here is to be honest with yourself. See yourself as a queen who is preparing for her king. You will attract what you are, not what you want. When I say "attract," I am not referring to all the guys who approach you; I am referring to the man who will be your partner for the long run. He will be a reflection of where you are, not where you want to be. So, become what you want to attract. Get your money up and your weight down if that is what you want in a man. Or get your weight up if that is what you desire in a man. Be in the best shape for you, and you will attract what you want in a man.

This requires a great deal of discipline, dedication and hard work. There will be tears at times, but the reward will be worth it. It is going to be difficult to put that pie down, or to avoid eating that ice cream, or to ignore the cheesecake, and pass on the fried foods. It will be expensive working with a skilled trainer, and the workouts will make you feel miserable at times in the middle of that set, but the results will be worthwhile.

Be healthy and fit for you! Be healthy and fit because you want to live a long life. Clinically, physical exercise releases chemicals like endorphins that aid in helping one to feel happy and positive. Work out for your peace of mind, and let the man it attracts be the bonus for all the hard work.

There you have it! The BRAIN, BRAND and BODY!! The 3 B's! Work on and perfect those 3 B's; the combination of these 3 B's can be a mechanism for truly loving yourself.

Beyond working on yourself inside and out, please understand that loving yourself is about being the best you and not compromising for anyone else. You cannot claim that getting in shape and being healthy are for someone else, because those things are for you. You cannot claim that building your brand and having something to call your own are for someone else, because those things are for you. You cannot claim that gaining knowledge of yourself and of love and relationships is for someone else, because that's for you.

But I'll tell you what *is* for someone else. Compromising your self-worth and self-respect is for someone else. If you have sex with a man because he asks or pressures you, that is compromising yourself. If he has not given you a ring and committed to you for life, then you do not owe him anything. If you have perfected the 3 B's, then a man will not expect you to compromise anything, because you're worth your weight in gold and more. He may ask you just to try it, but he does not expect you to compromise.

A compromise is sex before marriage. A compromise is loaning money to a grown man who is not your husband. A compromise is having a threesome or allowing your man to sleep with other women. A compromise is allowing your man to feed into lust like watching porn, going to strip clubs or the club in general. A compromise is allowing a man to yell at you, curse at you, belittle you and abuse you emotionally, verbally or physically.

A compromise is staying in a relationship with a man who lies to you over and over. A compromise is allowing a man to disrespect you or allowing his family or friends to disrespect you. A compromise is giving a second chance to a cheater, beater or manipulator. A compromise is financially supporting a man or letting him move in with you before marriage. A compromise is letting a man sit on his butt and chase fantasies while you work your fingers to the bones. A compromise is paying the bills when you have a grown, able-bodied man living with you. A compromise is living with a man or being with a man who indulges in illegal activities. A compromise is letting a man disrespect or neglect your children.

All of those things are compromises that are not worth making. If you compromise in any of those ways or anything similar, you do not love yourself yet. Stand your ground, know what you deserve, and accept nothing less. Love yourself!

What You
Need To
Know About
Love

L OVE, LOVE, LOVE! We all want true love, and we all need true love. True love finds us when we truly begin to love ourselves. You have read up to this point about how to truly love yourself, and now it is important to learn exactly what love is.

I travel the country every month to speak about love and relationships. I often ask members of my audience to raise their hands if they believe that love is pain. It never fails; at least half of the room raises their hands. I once thought that love was pain, too. That was my perception because that is what I had seen my whole life. I saw women being abused by their men. I saw men being abused by their women. I saw a lot of tears in relationships. I saw a lot of breakups. I saw a lot of sorrow and heartache. I thought that these were all aspects of "love." Then I realized about three years into my marriage that although pain is a part of many relationships, it is not actually a part of love.

I discovered that love has nothing to do with pain, and pain has nothing to do with love. We often call it "love" when we are in relationships, but just because you can have a relationship does not automatically mean you have love. There are many loveless relationships, and the people involved in them don't even know it. They get hurt in these relationships, and that is why they say love is pain. In actuality, the relationship is pain because neither party knows real love. Love is pure! Love is unselfish. Love understands. Love is patient. Love is kind. Love is forgiving. Love is giving. Love is selfless. Love is enduring. Love is sacrifice. Love is compromise. At no time does love equate with pain. Some people venture as far as to compare it to losing a loved one to death or to Jesus dying on the cross. I am neither referring to that type of love nor that type of pain. My point is in reference to the love that exists inside of an intimate relationship.

Many men drag pain into the love because they have never experienced real love. Many of us were raised around pimp-minded, abusive or cold men. Many of us were raised in environments that were so cold; we never learned how to be warm. So we enter into relationships and try to dominate women like we try to dominate in our sports. We try to control women because we are unable to control ourselves. We try to rule women but lack understanding of what really goes into the concept of leadership. We assume leadership is a dictatorship, when actually, it is service. We think that we are supposed to lead by force, when in actuality we are supposed to lead by example. We fail to realize that our greatest strength is in our gentleness. What's worse is that we have not learned how to balance the lion and the lamb cohabitating inside of us. We typically feed one and starve the other.

So if you have a man who does not know love, then he will be unable to show love. If he does not understand love, then he cannot give love. If he has never seen love, then he does not know what it looks like. Therefore, he goes into survival mode and -- when in survival mode – a man feels that he must oppress those around him in order to be in power. So he strips a woman of her dignity, pride and self-respect so that she is dependent on him in every aspect of her life. He breaks her to a point that she needs him in order to feel whole. He steals her mind and he controls her body. He does not fully understand why he is weakening his woman so that he can feel stronger. In his mind, he is doing what comes naturally or what he thinks he is supposed to do. He is trying to survive, but he fails to realize he is killing her slowly. Because he is hurting on the inside, he is hurting his woman.

I'm not making excuses for him; I am simply explaining to you why he does it. Most often, the man will not come into the knowledge of real love until a woman is strong enough to show him by example what love is, what love gives, and what love tolerates. When a woman learns to love herself, she then in return teaches the meaning of real love to every man who comes in contact with her. She ceases all behavior that is a result of self-hate, and she only reinforces behaviors of true love. She singlehandedly purifies the relationship and cultivates real love between herself and her man. A woman is the backbone, and she teaches a man how to love by the way she loves herself.

It was that lesson in love that changed me! My wife did not reinforce the toxic behaviors, so it forced me to learn new behaviors. If what came naturally did not work I had to do what did not come to me naturally, which was the opposite of my behaviors. She then reinforced those behaviors, and that is how I learned how to treat a woman – by what she stopped, what she allowed and what she reinforced.

If you don't know love, then someone will teach you how to hate yourself and then you will confuse the two!

It is imperative for you to know that love is not pampering. There is a difference between love and pampering. Just because a man pays for you to dress and look nice does not mean he loves you, and just because he does not do those things does not mean that he doesn't love you. Love is an idea and it is based on actions, but those actions are intangible actions. Love is how he talks to you, how he respects you, how he treats you. Love is not how much he can spend on you or how much he does for you. A player and a pimp know how to do and say all the right things when they need to, but that does not mean the player or pimp loves you any more than sitting in a garage will make you a car.

If it's painful, it's not love. In an intimate relationship, there is a fine line between love and pain. It may hurt you that you cannot go on a shopping spree, but that is not the type of pain I am referencing. The pain I'm referring to originates from infidelity, verbal abuse, emotional abuse and physical abuse. A man who curses you out like a dog does not love you. A man who continues to cheat on you – even after you have caught him and expressed your hurt and pain – does not love you. A man who talks down to you, disrespects you or puts his hands on you does not love you. Some women think that it's possible for a man to do those things and still love his woman. No, that is not possible. Love and hate cannot reside in the same space.

Think about it from this perspective: If he hits you, does he hit his mom? He does not hit his mom because he loves her! He has been angry with her too, but he does not resort to hitting her or cursing her because he loves her! He hits you and curses you because he does not love you. If he does hit or curse both you and his mom, then that means he is full of hate, anger and rage. He is incapable of love at this point in his life because he hates himself. You must understand that love has fruit and hate has fruit. Love is a good tree and hate is a bad tree. A good tree will not produce bad fruit and a bad tree will not produce good fruit. The difference about a human and a tree is that a human can be dug up, reworked at the roots, and replanted again to produce good fruit. What that means is that if your man does not know love, then you may have to let him go so he can grow!

If "love" is hurting you, then something is wrong. If you are crying more than you're smiling, then something is wrong. If you are afraid of your partner, then something is wrong. If you have to walk on eggshells, then something is wrong. If you cannot have friends and cannot be close to your family, then something is wrong. I just want to dispel all myths that love is pain, because it is not. I am not suggesting that you seek out a fairytale, but know that love should not cause you hurt, sorrow, pain or misery.

I am living this, so this is why I'm teaching it. In my relationship with my wife we have disagreements, but we don't argue. If I upset her or she upsets me, we talk about it and we move on. I do not call her out of her name or beat her conscience into the ground. I do not harp on it for days. We talk about it for an hour at the most, then we cool off, right our wrongs within ourselves and we start fresh. We do not yell, scream, or curse under any circumstances! I have never cursed at my wife and she has never cursed at me. I have never hit my wife or ripped her to pieces by calling her ugly names.

After we learned what real love is, our lives changed. Before we started truly loving each other, there were tears and many arguments. Then I began to study real love through Jesus Christ, and I began to love my wife the way Christ loves the church. It changed me and it changed her. We began to put one another first. My goal is to please her in every way, and her goal is to please me in every way. I am looking out for her best interest in all things, and she is looking out for my best interest in all things. We became selfless instead of selfish. We became compassionate instead of confrontational. We seek to understand instead of being understood. We seek to give instead of take. We choose to forgive and forget instead of harboring hate, anger and resentment.

Those changes have changed us tremendously, and I can now say I truly know what it means to love and to be loved. I want everyone to experience this peace and this joy, and that is why I have dedicated my life to sharing real love in this world. Once you know love and you experience love you will never want to settle for anything less. But in order to get love, you have to know what it is, know how to give it, and know how to accept it from others. Loving others does not mean letting them run over you. Loving others means giving them love and making sure they give you the same thing in return; if they don't, loving them means letting them go!

What You Need To Know About A Relationship

I F YOU ARE single or headed toward being single, then it's obvious that something has not gone quite right in your relationships. It is not always your fault, and it may have never been your fault. By now you probably know all about a bad relationship and some things that can ruin a relationship, but you have yet to experience a relationship that works so you may not fully understand what that takes. Some of the things that I hear single people ask for in relationships are just not realistic because no one is perfect; you will never have 100% of what you originally wanted in a person. You can learn to love them for 100% of who they are and change your wish list to read exactly what they are, but I'm sure that will not be the same list you wrote while you were single and in waiting. There will always be a compromise, but it must be a healthy compromise. You must never compromise your self-respect.

A relationship is the hardest thing to make-work because it is composed of two naturally selfish human beings, both trying to change the other person to fit what they want. For the longest, a relationship is a battle of the wills. Both parties are inadvertently trying to change the other person. Sometimes one person wins and they have this shell of a person who they think is right for them, but even that won't last because the other person gets tired of being someone they're not. A relationship, as you know, is a give and take. You give some and you get some. The question is, what should you give and what should you get? I'll use my relationship as an example because it is the only one that I have been able to make-work. Since we have the formula seven years in, I do not think we will ever get divorced unless one of us takes a "stupid pill" or bumps our head somewhere. God forbid!

My wife is my complete opposite! She loves to laugh, joke, play around and is very outgoing. She loves roller coasters, the outdoors, the beach and adventures. She can go all day long and still have energy. We were once at Disney World for 17 hours and she still wasn't complaining. I just really do not understand how she does it. If we wrestle together, she will never tap out or say she's tired or has had enough. My wife will literally play fight until the house is burned down or one of us is in the hospital if I let her. When I say that, I'm being completely serious. There is a kid in her that will just stay young forever. Truth be told, my wife is only 26 and that kid in her is like six.

At the same time she is very mature for her age, and sometimes I forget how young she is because of her conversational skills and her ability to manage our finances and my businesses while being an amazing mother. I am 29 years old, and I feel like a 65-year-old. I am very laid back and relaxed. I like to smile and laugh but only at comedy shows. I am very serious about life, and I'm always thinking about business and my purpose in life. I am highly motivated in business, which is why I have created 23 streams of income before the age of 30.

A perfect day for me is one like today where I slept in late, woke up and washed up, and then got back in bed to work on my computer. Then I'd love to eat dinner with my family, kick back and watch a movie after my son is put to bed. Nowhere in there do I want to play fight, wrestle or pull practical jokes like my wife would love to do. But we have learned to compromise! If I was unwilling to compromise, she would drive me insane. I would bore her to death if *she* weren't willing to compromise. I compromise when I tell subtle jokes and she cracks up laughing. I don't even crack a smile, but she's bent over laughing. She doesn't know it but whenever she laughs at my jokes, I already know she's going to laugh at them and I've set them up for her to laugh. She thinks she's just getting a laugh off of me, but I'm making that face or saying that thing just to make her laugh. Then I may start a play fight with her just so she can get it out of her system. I let it go on for five minutes or so and then I tap out, or else I'd end up in the hospital or accidently hurt her trying to defend myself.

After the play fight, she will take a "chill pill" and watch a boring documentary with me just to please me. Then we go to sleep and repeat it the next day. She lets me sleep in because I have worked hard enough to afford some extra sleep on some days, and she lets me stay up late working because she knows I work best when it's absolute quiet and in the still of the night. She does not wake me up and she does not force me to go to sleep.

I let her shop even when I don't think she really needs to, and I let her buy things that mean something to her and absolutely nothing to me. I let her go out to lunch or brunch with her girlfriends, and I do not worry about her whereabouts or if she's bad-mouthing me or not. My wife cooks and cleans when she wants to and I do not make her do otherwise. If she doesn't feel like cleaning up or cooking, then I'll step over the junk and go out to buy us dinner. I understand that she is a human being and not a robot, and that just like I don't want to cook and clean every day, neither does she. Sometimes, I leave the toilet seat up and my underwear in the middle of the floor. I leave my finished plate on the table and my used stuff out on the counter. She does not nag me about it; she picks it up without my ever knowing that I even left it. She subtly mentions it later, but not in an argumentative way, just as a passing joke. We have learned that not everything needs to be said and not every issue is a problem. We have learned not to sweat the little stuff and that if it's not worth breaking up over, then it's not worth arguing over. We may mention it in a conversation and hope that we both catch the hints and do better, but even if we don't, we don't lose sleep over it.

Right now my wife is pregnant, and she hinted the other day that she needed some help around the house.

The house looks the way it always does but – where she used to find some energy to clean it – now she doesn't have that same type of energy. I told her I would drive our son to school in the morning, but because I have been sleeping past that point and she lets me, I decided to start doing the cooking and cleaning. One thing she can't stand is washing the dishes, so now I cook and then wash the dishes afterwards. I realized that I actually like the peace and solace I find while cooking and doing dishes, so it's something I plan to continue even after our new baby arrives. My wife still does the laundry though. I appreciate her for that. When she's not able to, I'll do it, and I may find out that I like that as well.

There may come a day when I need to wake up early to take my son to school, return home to take my wife to a doctor's appointment, coach my clients, do my own work, pick my son up from school, cook dinner, and then wash the dishes. Guess what? Because I know real love and what a real relationship is, I'll do it all with pride. I know that if the tables were turned, my wife would do the same thing for me.

I have come to realize that's what a relationship is about, healthy compromise. I'm not asking my wife to believe that every man cheats and to let me cheat. I'm not asking my wife to let me go to the strip club and indulge in porn. I'm not asking my wife engage in a threesome to fulfill a fantasy for me. I'm not asking my wife to cut off her friends and family and let me be her everything. I'm not asking my wife to accept my temper tantrums and understand that if I beat her, it's because I love her. I'm not asking my wife to let me curse her out when I get mad and do what I want when I want because I'm a man! I'm not asking her to do those things! Those are ludicrous. That is not love, and it is not a real relationship. If you allow a man to do those things, you're not in a relationship. You're in slavery.

My wife does not want to leave me over a toilet seat being left up, nor does she start World War III over petty things like that. She doesn't nag me about the insignificant things. If she needs something, she asks for it. She does not steal money and misuse it buying useless junk. She is not asking me to pamper her like a princess, and if money is tight, she rolls with the punches of life. She doesn't add stress; she helps relieve the stress. If she has to step up in any way, then she will do so. She helps me stay on track and focused, instead of stealing my focus and stressing me out.

She is not jealous or insecure. She doesn't question me about text messages, Facebook, Instagram or Twitter. She does not hound me when I'm on the road. She trusts me and gives me enough rope to hang myself or help myself. The choice is mine. She does not force my hand. She treats me with so much respect and honor that I have no desire to cheat. I want to come home to her. If the thought of cheating crosses my mind at this point in our relationship, it breaks my heart to picture the aftermath of it.

It took us about 2-3 years to reach that point, but once we did, we never looked back. I want you to know that in those 2-3 years, there was no open cheating, beating or blatant disrespect. There were unnecessary arguments and unnecessary attitudes, and that's it. You should never tolerate behavior that can be harmful to your mental, physical, emotional or spiritual well-being. If it's destructive, then leave. If your partner wants you back, they can work for you and prove that they are ready and willing do it the right way.

In a healthy relationship there are no gender roles, and both parties must understand that. A woman can be the breadwinner just like the man can cook and clean. Both parties must be mature enough to accept what comes with a relationship. I thought a woman was supposed to do everything in a home, but I learned that I may have to and that I needed to do so with a smile on my face. There was a time when my wife made $5/hour more than me, and we were working for the same company. It was upsetting some days, but I had to get over my ego. What's remarkable about it is that even though she made more money than me, she never rubbed it in my face or spent the money how she wanted to spend it. She brought it all to the table and let me lead as the man by deciding where the money needed to be spent first. As a man, I had to consider her needs as a woman and not be selfish, stingy, greedy or vindictive. There are many men who cannot handle a woman earning more, and as a result of their own insecurities hurt their relationships with their temper tantrums or selfish spending habits. If a man cannot handle that a woman makes more than him, then he needs to let her go.

I was a young kid when I said a relationship is 50/50. Then my cousin said, *"No it's not. It's 51/49 because someone has to be the bigger person when a decision needs to be made."* We were literally no older than 15 years old. I'm sure he heard that logic from his mom or dad, who were both great parents. That has always stuck with me, because it was not often that one of my peers schooled me on something serious. I realized the truth in that because there are those times where someone has to step up and be the bigger person. That responsibility transfers sometimes from day to day. Today, it may be the woman compromising, and tomorrow it may be the man compromising. Either way, a compromise must be made.

A relationship is a team! For the men reading this, I want you to understand that your woman is an asset, not a liability. She is for you, not against you. Stop trying to control and demean your woman; build her up instead! Empower your woman and let her be a woman. Her brain is stronger than yours and she uses both sides of her brain whereas men only use one side. Let her add to your life instead of shutting her down and weakening your team. God made her to help, not to hurt. She is born to love and created to be a helpmeet. Let her help you!

Please know that you cannot lead her if you are not following God. Also know that a leader is a servant! Serve and lead by example, and she will follow. If you treat her like a queen, protecting and providing and she's still not reciprocating, then you have chosen the wrong woman and must let her go!

Ladies, support your man! Encourage him and speak into his life. Don't nag about every little thing. Embrace his flaws and ask him to embrace yours. Flaws are little things that really have no bearing on the relationship. The world has beaten him up enough; he needs you to speak life over him and lift him up. Hold him accountable, and don't accept any nonsense from him. Force him to step up and be a man even when he's afraid to do so. If he will not respect you or treat you the way you deserve to be treated, then he must be let go!

Don't Be Afraid To Be Single

I F YOU ARE afraid to be single, you have to evaluate why. Many times we get comfortable in relationships, and even when they hurt us so badly we cannot seem to let go. I am not a therapist, but life has taught me that people typically do not want to be single because they have not fully matured as individuals. The average person typically relies on someone else to feel whole. We are lost and afraid in this big world. You may be hurting from your past and think you need someone to be there to help take away the pain. You may miss your mother or father or someone you loved or wanted to love and a relationship seems to fill that void. You may be afraid of breaking up because you don't want to please the haters. You may be afraid of embarrassment. You may feel afraid of letting your friends and family down. You may feel like people will secretly make fun of you for your failed relationship.

You might even feel afraid of starting all over again. You might fear never being able to find anyone else to understand you the way the one you are already with has learned to understand you. You may be afraid of being a failure at love. Perhaps you feel you are in too deep to leave. Perhaps you feel you have come too far to turn back. You may feel you suffered through too much to let someone else reap the benefits of your hard work. You may even be afraid that the next person will get the best version of your partner. Yes, I get it!

But even though I get it, none of those reasons are enough for anyone to remain in a bad relationship. You have to be able to heal on your own. You may need counseling, therapy and life coaching, but you have to be willing to heal on your own. You have to grow comfortable with being alone and learn to truly love yourself. While you are clinging to a toxic relationship and going back and forth trying to force it to work, you could be missing the person of your dreams. The person of your dreams could be watching you every day, but you are so focused on your toxic lover that you can't even see them. As the saying goes, "You cannot move on to the next if you're still focused on your ex."

You have to decide that enough is enough. If you have left for a period of time, returned to the relationship and the person still hasn't changed, then you must realize that they may never change. If a person is going to change, it should only take you leaving them once. If you leave once for at least 24 hours and then you come back and that person hasn't changed, then they may never change. Maybe you left for a week or more and then returned, and before long, your partner returned to their old ways. I know that happens often. Most of the time, this happens because your partner does not believe that you love yourself enough to leave forever.

This person knows that you need them to fill a void in your life and – no matter how tough you want to appear – you will always come back. Once your partner has figured that out, then it's over for your happiness. At that point, your partner owns you. You must reclaim your independence and learn to love yourself whole-heartedly.

If you reflect and realize that you have been in back-to-back relationships ever since you started dating, then something is wrong. You have missed the opportunity to be single, to learn and to grow while single. If you're in a toxic relationship right now and your last relationship was toxic as well, that's another sign to which you should take heed. It's time to break free! It's time to learn how to start over and do it the right way. Don't get trapped in a burning house. You staying in a toxic relationship is the same as you staying in a burning house; eventually it will consume you! You have to be willing to escape, even if that means leaving with nothing and starting fresh. If you got it once then you can get it again, but the next time you can do it better. Love won't run from you. You will attract love again, but this time you will attract pure love because you'll be ready for it. You will have done all that you need to do while single.

Have the faith and the courage to leave that broken relationship and you will discover a peace like never before. I have coached many people who needed coaching before they left their toxic relationships. After they left is when the divine happened. That is when a person can enter a space of peace and wholeness and begin to birth things that had been aborted before. In that space you can birth hobbies, new companies, new missions, and a sense of purpose. In that space, I have seen people attract new friends and notice potential partners that they would have overlooked in the past.

There becomes an infatuation with single life and the peace and joy it can bring when you truly fall in love with yourself. There are many singles today who are 100% happy and satisfied with single life. They realize that it is better to be alone than to be in the wrong relationship. That is the mindset you need to adopt if you find yourself trapped, dealing with a toxic lover. Maybe you do not live with this person. Maybe you are on and off. Maybe you are on a break right now, but are strongly considering going back. Maybe you are trying to leave, but they keep calling you every day making promises. No matter what it is, you have to make up in your mind that if it was not right before and you have given it every chance to succeed, then it's probably still not going to be right.

In baseball, you only get 3 strikes before you're out. In basketball, you only get 2 technical fouls before you are tossed out of the game. And in every game, you are only allowed a certain amount of timeouts. A relationship is a very serious game, and you're playing for keeps. You're playing for hearts. You are not really "playing" in the typical sense of the word, but the philosophy is the same. Even in the relationship game, there should be strict rules. You should not be able to take unlimited breaks. There should not be multiple technical fouls or strikes. You must have limits and boundaries and

– when you've reached them – it is time for repercussions. One repercussion is leaving.

Now you know how to discover the beauty of single life and all the things that you should be doing, but if you are in a toxic relationship of any form, then I really want you to confront yourself and decide that you deserve better. There are good people in the world who are ready to love you and will appreciate you for all that you're worth. There are people waiting on you to wake up and smell the coffee and realize that you deserve so much more than you're settling for in this negative relationship. If you keep settling for what you have, then one day you will forget what you actually deserve. If you are with a toxic lover, then that person will eventually make you feel like you deserve exactly what they are giving you. Do not confuse their self-hate as love for you. They don't love you if they're mistreating you! They hate themselves if they're mistreating you, and you must realize that.

It's possible that you made a mistake. Just because you ended up in a relationship with someone does not mean that it was meant to be. Sometimes certain happenings in life are just meant to be lessons for a season, not a lifetime. It is possible that by not knowing love and how to love yourself, you allowed someone who could not love you get close to you. You have to recognize that mistake and make changes. Just because you made a mistake does not mean you have to live in it. You can get up, and you can leave!

Heal Before You Deal

HEALING IS OF the essence. You must heal while you are single. You may need counseling. You may need therapy. You may need a life coach. Depending on what you've been through, you have to decide what level of help you need. We all need some type of help. Do not trick yourself into believing that getting help means that you're sick in the head or that your life is pathetic. Getting help means that you are on the right track. It means that you are loving and investing in yourself in the present to prepare for a better future.

A lot of people do not heal in between relationships; therefore, they continue to cause or endure pain. Is that you? Are you holding on to the abandonment of your father? Are you holding on to the abuse you suffered at the hands of a loved one? Are you still recovering from being raped or molested? Are you jaded because of a past relationship? Do you think all men are dogs? Do you feel that no woman can be trusted? Do you feel that love is pain? Do you feel that marriage is outdated and no longer necessary? Do you feel that love is a lost art?

If you answered "Yes" to any of those things, that's a sign that you need to heal. We believe the things we believe because of what we have witnessed or experienced in our lifetime. Just because we have lived it or have seen it does not mean that it's the only way. Just because it happened to you does not mean you have to hold on to it for life or relive it over and over again. You can overcome your past. You can rewrite your future. You can change your life and heal your heart. You must heal before you deal.

You have heard of the term "baggage." We all carry around some type of baggage with the hopes that we will meet someone who will help us carry that baggage or unpack it. To expect that of any human is unfair because they will most likely have baggage of their own. So instead, what you must do is unpack your personal baggage before you meet someone and hope that they have unpacked theirs. If they haven't, then you will easily notice it and be able to speak into their lives and testify about what you have been able to do. If not, the baggage will clutter the relationship, and it could be the reason the relationship fails. Unpack the baggage!!

If you need to learn what love is and what you deserve in a relationship, then you need a life coach. If you need to heal from mommy or daddy wounds or wounds of the past from molestation, rape, pain, abandonment, etc., then you need a therapist. Understand your needs and meet them, because you cannot expect anyone else to meet them for you.

I remember that after I left a toxic relationship, I did not take time to heal and I ruined my next relationship. In one relationship, I was a cheater, a liar, a manipulator and controlling. I left that relationship because I hated the way it made me feel, but I did not seek help to fix those behaviors. In the next relationship, I pushed the woman away. The next woman was my wife.

I came into the relationship playing a role of what I figured she wanted to see and hear, but before I knew it, I was trying to control and run her life. She let me go less than two months into the relationship. I did not get another shot to make it work until six months later. I had learned from my mistakes, but there was still a lot more I needed to fix in myself that I hadn't. I ended up having to fix it in the relationship, and I almost cost myself the relationship again. I had to heal from growing up soft and being pushed around. There were fights as a young man that I should have fought even if I would have lost them. Those beatings would've made me more of a man, because at least I would have had the contentment of knowing that I stood my ground. Many times, I walked away from fights and then carried that anger with me all of my life.

Inside of my relationships, when I realized that I was with a weaker individual, I would try to find opportunities to blow up and try to get out that anger that had been suppressed for so many years. I needed help! I needed to learn how to channel that anger and release it in a positive way. I needed to learn how to not let the anger get the best of me and how to beat it. This is the healing that I needed. I worked with my father, who is a professional life coach and advisor. He taught me how to be a man and how to love. He taught me everything that love is and how to handle myself in frustrating situations inside of a relationship. For the first time, he could really transfer this knowledge to me, and I was ready to receive it.

I listened to everything he taught me, and I implemented those lessons into my life. I also coupled his wisdom with the wisdom of Jesus Christ, Zig Ziglar and Dr. Gary Chapman. Their wisdom helped me become a man who really knew how to love. Unlike most men I am not afraid or ashamed to give credit where credit is due, and even to acknowledge the impact that complete strangers have had on my life. That was when I began to heal, and it changed me forever.

Look back over your life and make a mark about anything that has ever hurt you. If it hurt you and you never talked it through with someone who possesses real wisdom, then it is probably still affecting you today. You have to confront those incidents in your past and heal from them so that you can move forward as a healthy and productive individual in love and in life. I notice a lot of people suffering in love because of something they have experienced in their past. It's usually pain that stemmed from a mother or father. If it's not pain, then it's ignorance they gained from their mother, father or someone they loved and emulated.

I see a lot of men who cannot love women the way they deserve because of a father who couldn't love, and the father failed to love because of the way *he* was raised or unloved, so it just gets passed down from generation to generation. If "love" is hurting you, or if your "love" is hurting someone else, then something needs to be fixed! You must question the lessons you have received about love over the years and learn real love.

Typically, I find that my clients do not have real love because they are being selfish. Many of them desire love from their partners, but have no idea how to reciprocate that love. Other than that, I find that many people do not believe in love today and feel that it's overrated. They only feel that way because they have never received real love before. There is always a reason and a solution. There is always a reason why a person is unable to love or receive love. There is always a solution to it as well. The solution, most times, is something most people do not want to hear or are afraid to confront. The solution can be simple, but it won't be easy.

No matter what you have suffered through, you have to realize that there is a purpose in it. It did not happen to you because you deserved it. It happened to you because you can survive it and do something with it. Your pain can birth your purpose, and you can change lives with your story. You can prevent other people from going through what you experienced. That is my purpose in writing this book, because my pain birthed it. You can do the same in whatever form you wish. Maybe you can write a book, start a foundation, become a speaker or become a blogger. There is a purpose in your pain and you have to find it.

Healing is mandatory. Forgiveness is something you do for yourself, as well as for the person who hurt you. You have to let the hurt, pain and anger motivate you to do something great with your story. You cannot allow it to beat you up or cause you to beat others up. You have to beat it. You beat it by fighting back with a will to inspire others. You can change the lives of others with the knowledge and wisdom you have gained from your life. You can fight the pain back, and you can win. You fight it by obtaining new knowledge of self. You fight it by seeking help. You fight it by investing in yourself and your dreams and being committed to changing lives. Do not continue to hurt yourself or to hurt others. End the cycle of blocking love or hindering love because of your pain.

When you are hurting from your past, people can see it even when you think you have masked it. People can see it in your smile, hear it in your laugh, feel it in your tone, and sense it in your conversation. When you are hurting from your past, the pain has a way of seeping into your everyday life. You have to identify it and heal it and not just run from it. Change your life. Heal your pain and attract real love.

Make up in your mind today that you will hire a life coach, counselor or therapist to deal with whatever issues you may have to confront, no matter how big or small they seem. If you are a prayer warrior, then start praying on it daily. Have a coach help you turn your pain into purpose and help save others some trouble. Make up in your mind that you will no longer be a victim to your past and present circumstances, but that you will be a victor and will defeat your pain.

It is time to love you and to work on yourself. Let all toxic love go and prepare for real love. You teach people how to treat you by how you treat yourself. If you accept it, then people will continue to give it to you. You don't get what you deserve, you get what you demand. You have to get yours by first getting your life. Get your life! Claim your happiness! Claim your peace! Claim your joy! Claim your healing! Claim your love!

Your time is now! Make something beautiful happen!

CPSIA information can be obtained at www.ICGtesting.com
Printed in the USA
LVOW05s0230180214

374126LV00011B/82/P